Easy To Read

Poems For Children

written by HELENE BARNES

photographed by VERNON BARNES

Order this book online at www.trafford.com
or email orders@trafford.com

Most Trafford titles are also available at major online book retailers.

Print information available on the last page.

ISBN: 978-1-4120-3972-7 (sc)
        978-1-4907-2950-3 (e)

Trafford rev. 08/06/2018

www.trafford.com

North America & international
toll-free: 1 888 232 4444 (USA & Canada)
fax: 812 355 4082

Dedicated to my parents for their devotion,
support and so many happy childhood memories.
Also, for teaching me compassion.

THE PET STORE

Hi, I saw you looking at me.
Aren't I cute?
Why not take me home?
I'm a Pekinese.
In this cage, I feel alone.
Take me with you please.

You're just the child that I need.
You can cuddle with this toy breed.
I'm not the prettiest,
But loyal and devoted.
Tell your parents,
Put me on your birthday list.

You stare at me,
You see in my eyes
A human quality,
A heart that feels, cries.
Revealing loneliness, sadness.
Because there is no one to love me.

Oh fantastic!
She's opening the door,
Taking me home,
I'm loved,
Alone no more.

SHEEP

Sheep grazing in the meadow,
Baby lambs jump and play.
Sheep dog keeps them from going astray.

Here comes grandpa with dinner.
They come running when he calls,
They push and shove,
Not well mannered at all.

Baa baa they bleat,
"Corn kernels,
What a treat."

Three baby lambs,
Five sheep and a ram.
The ram is a male,
He's got small horns and a tail.

Sheep stay cool under the willow,
When grandpa leaves, they follow,
All in a row, off they go.

PIRATE

Pirate book I read,
Then I went to bed,
Had a dream.
I was a pirate,
A patch on my eye,
Hat on my head.

Treasure, pirate ship,
Walking a plank,
Storms, sails that rip.
Ship that sank.

Cannon fire,
Sword fights.
Adventures on the seas,
"Wake up, its light."

I'm glad it was a dream.
The ship was sinking,
I started to scream.
I'd rather be an optometrist.
It's honorable and safe,
No fight with swords and fist.

FLOWER GIRLS

Grandma made wreaths for our hair,
And white dresses she told us not to tear.
When we got the cue,
We remembered what to do.

We walked down the aisle in front of the bride,
Guests were sitting on either side.
We threw rose petals,
Mom said we did well.

We stood with the bridesmaids in a row.
They wore fancy gowns with a bow.
The groom wore a tuxedo.

My brother carried a small pillow.
On it was the wedding ring.
A lady playing a harp began to sing.

At the reception
We danced and ate cake.
It was outdoors by the lake.
Relatives had fun, uncles and aunts,
Some came all the way from France.

Presents were piled high,
China, silver, crystal dishes,
Wedding cards with best wishes.

We liked being flower girls,
We liked wearing necklaces of pearls.
New shoes made of leather,
Our family being all together.

Dancing With Dolphins

Moving in the sea,
Just you and me,
Together, in harmony,
Dancing with a dolphin.

I have to go,
But this memory will stay.
Even when I grow
Very old and grey,
I'll still remember
Dancing with a dolphin.

CREEPY, CRAWLY THINGS

My brother likes creepy crawly things.
Not me, I like dolls and rings.
I don't like snakes and bugs.
I don't like slimy slugs.

My brother likes creepy crawly things.
He plays with lizards and caterpillars.
That's what my brother enjoys.
Me, I prefer my toys.

My brother likes creepy, crawly things.
Me, I prefer to play Queen and Kings.
I wear a silver crown
And a beautiful gown.

SEBASTIAN

My name is Sebastian.
I like to win
At checkers and chess,
At ping pong and croquet,
At any game I play.

I have gold fish and a guppy,
A turtle and a Husky.
I take care of my pets.
It teaches me responsibility.

I like to collect stamps
And go to Boy Scout Camp.
Hiking on trails,
Picking raspberries
With our pails.

In summer,
I lie on the deck,
Stare up at the sky,
Watching the clouds go by,
Big, puffy cumulus,
Whispy cirrus.

My grandma reads me a story,
About an elephant named Dori,
Then I say my prayers before I sleep,
Pray to God, my soul to keep.

TENNIS

Tennis is my sport.
Playing on a court,
Serving with my racket,
Here comes the ball, hit.

When I grow up,
I will compete.
Coach says
I'm fast on my feet.
In a tournament,
Difficult to beat.

Winter

In the morning,
Looking out the window,
The dreary landscape
Became a fresh, white drape
Of bright, sparkling ice and snow.

The lights twinkled upon the roof tops.
Smell of cookies baking,
The carolers begin to sing.
For gifts the people shop.

Under the tree, children find a toy.
The family comes together,
Despite the nasty weather.
The mood is one of joy.

We'd skate until our feet were numb,
Then defrost in front of the fire.
Snuggling in our warm beds we'd retire,
Hoping in the night Santa will come.

The snowman starts to melt,
His nose and hat upon the ground.
Silent night, not a sound,
And mother's love we always felt.

Ivy The Cat

My pet is a cat.
Her name is Ivy.
Prettiest cat you ever did see.
Ivy cleans her paws and fur,
Curls up and starts to purr.

Sitting on the window sill,
Looking out the window,
Watching a whippoorwhil.

"Meow, Meow,
Where is my dinner?
Fish is my favorite,
But I'll settle for cat chow."

LEAVES

Pile of leaves,
Fallen from trees,
Gold, orange, red,
I made a bed.

Red Cardinal

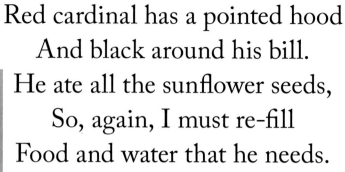

Red cardinal has a pointed hood
And black around his bill.
He ate all the sunflower seeds,
So, again, I must re-fill
Food and water that he needs.

Winter has come.
The leaves have fallen.
Ice covers the branches
Crystal, glimmering ice.
His feathers keep him warm
During a cold winter storm.
His bright red color contrasts
Against the white snow.
Where will he sleep tonight
When the cold winds blow?

Spider Web

Oh no,
I'm caught in a spider's web
And can't get out.
It's sticky and I'm trapped.
What a day!
I went the wrong way.
Now, I'll be his lunch.
Crunch, crunch.

THE SEA

Full of life and wonder,
Waves pounding,
Graceful sea gulls,
Over the sea flying.
Coral, crabs, shells,
Fish, seaweed and algae,
All this and more,
We find in the sea.
On the horizon,
Shrimp boats sail.
Oh look, there goes a whale!

FRIENDS

Friends will listen.
Friends will care.
Friends will give.
Friends will share.

A friend is someone
In whom you can confide.
In difficult times,
They don't leave your side.

A true friend is loyal.
They don't have to be rich.
They don't have to be royal.

Someone you can talk to,
If you're sad.
Secrets they can keep,
Even in their sleep.

Mr. Squirrel

Mr. Squirrel,
Eating sunflower seeds.
Go away!
Those are for the birds to feed.

Don't you know
It's wrong to steal
For your meal?

Every day
I chase him away.
Every day
He returns.

I caught him
In a cage,
Took him to the park.
Now he hunts for acorns,
From morn to dark.

CAMPING

We piled into the station wagon
And drove up the mountain.
We packed all the camping equipment,
Cooking supplies, flashlights and tent.

A canopy so we don't get wet.
A mosquito net
So we don't get bit.
Don't forget the first aid kit.

Put the hooks into the ground.
Get the hammer,
Pound, pound, pound.
Choose a spot that's flat.
Put down the blankets and mat.

Collect the wood for a fire.
Dry leaves first, then tinder,
Kindling and logs.
Light it and blow.
Flames keep us warm, glow.

The fire dies down.
Silence, not a sound.
The embers burn orange, blue.
Shining bright, colored hues.

In the woods,
Close to nature,
Material things, I don't miss.
I feel closer to God,
More happiness.

See the stars so clear and bright.
See the constellations in the night.
Smell the air, fresh and clean.
Time for bed, sweet dreams.

Printed in the United States
By Bookmasters

ISBN 978-1-4120-3972-7

51278

9 781412 039727